02/22

D1709588

Tales of the Rails

Legendary Train Routes of the World

Illustrated by Ryan Johnson
Written by Nathaniel Adams

LITTLE
GESTALTEN

Journeys

Alaska Railroad 52

48 Rocky Mountaineer

NORTH AMERICA

64 New York & Atlantic Railway

All aboard!

There are many good reasons to use trains today. They help connect cities, towns, and communities with each other and their inhabitants with the land around them. They are a safe and reliable form of transportation. And they are better for the environment than airplanes and cars because they can transport greater numbers of people and goods while using less fuel.

There are so many different kinds of trains: tourist trains with glass-topped observation cars for seeing the landscape; high-speed commuter trains that bring people from their homes to their jobs; sleeper trains for hotel-on-rails vacations; and freight trains that carry food, fuel, and materials that we all use in daily life. Railways are used all over the world—they span mountain ranges, tunnel under harbors, zip through cities, and cross plains, deserts, and forests.

Trains are almost as diverse as the people who ride them! This book will show you just a few special services operating in the world today and introduce you to some of the people who ride and work on them, as well as the sights you can see from their windows. Rail travel is fun and exciting; let's take a ride!

SOUTH AMERICA

58 PeruRail

Words marked with an asterisk* are explained in the glossary, p. 70.

3

Bernina Railway & Glacier Express
Crossing the Snowy Swiss Alps

The Matterhorn

The Landwasser Viaduct, which is part of the Glacier Express's route, was built 1901–1902. It is raised on six limestone arches that are 213 feet (65 meters) high.

The Bernina railway and the Glacier Express both cross the Swiss Alps, but head in opposite directions, following routes that take them through different altitudes and climates. When you travel on the Bernina Express you can see both mountains and palm trees, and in the winter, the Bernina railway often uses a snowplow that is more than 100 years old.

The Glacier Express runs from Zermatt at the foot of the Matterhorn to Saint Moritz, and the Bernina railway from Saint Moritz to Tirano in Italy. The Glacier Express also has a famously steep route that can give some people butterflies in their stomach!

Both routes are famous for the unforgettable views of mountains and engineering marvels, including beautiful tunnels and viaducts*—the Bernina railway even travels over a nine-arched spiral viaduct. The most impressive mountain is the Matterhorn, which is 14,692 feet (4,478 meters) high and famous for being one of the most difficult to climb because of its sheer faces. It used to be possible to see at least one glacier (a large sheet of ice) from the Glacier Express, but now, partly because of route changes and partly because climate change has shrunk the glaciers, they don't come as far down the mountains as they once did.

If you travel on the full route of the Bernina Express, you will cross 196 bridges and go through 55 tunnels.

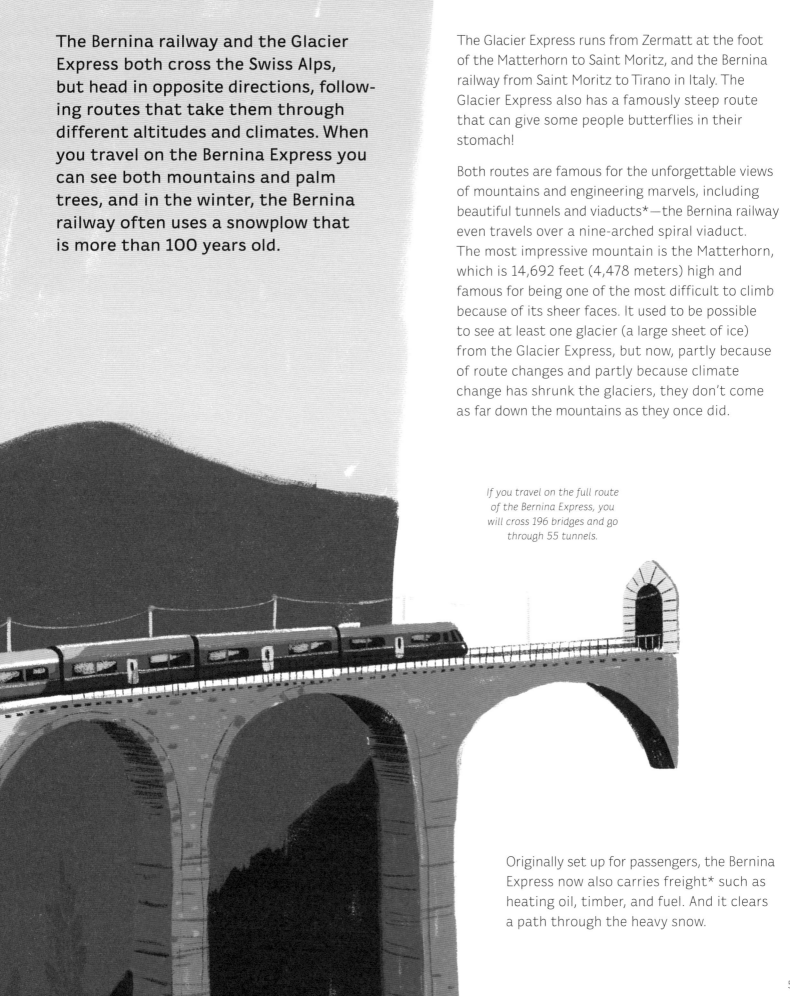

Originally set up for passengers, the Bernina Express now also carries freight* such as heating oil, timber, and fuel. And it clears a path through the heavy snow.

The rotary snowplow of the Bernina Express is a big and sharp metal wheel attached to the front of the train's engine during the winter months that spins round, cutting through ice and moving snow out of the way.

The plow uses energy from the locomotive's fuel source to spin the sharp-bladed wheel.

Before the rotary plow was introduced, locomotives* in snowy areas had large wedges attached to their fronts that would push the snow to the sides as they drove through it.

However, this didn't work well for very thickly packed or ice-hard snow, and the train had to move very fast to have enough energy to push the snow aside, which could be dangerous on icy mountains.

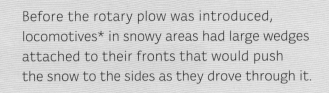

The sharp-bladed wheel chops up the snow and ice.

The chopped-up snow and ice is fired out of a chute, high up into the air.

It falls on the banks farther from the track than if it were simply pushed out of the way.

The rotary snowplow was first invented in 1869 by a dentist—not so surprising, considering how much drilling they have to do!

The Glacier Express is known as the world's slowest express train because, despite its name, it is meant for leisurely sightseeing over an eight-hour journey.

René's family loves to ski, and one of their favorite places to do that is at the famous resort of Saint Moritz. Here they are getting ready to board the Glacier Express for their ski holiday. And off they go!

Caledonian Sleeper & the Jacobite

Take Britain's Famous Sleeper Train, Then Travel by Steam

The Jacobite, a steam-engine passenger service that runs over what many people say is one of the most scenic rail routes in the world—the Mallaig Extension— departs from Fort William, Scotland. Getting there from the U.K.'s capital city, London, is an adventure in itself when you travel by the Caledonian Sleeper.

VALID ONLY WITH RESERVATIONS

COUNTRY: the U.K.

LENGTH: London Euston to Fort William, about 415 miles (668 kilometers); Mallaig Extension, 42 miles (68 kilometers)

MAIN STOPS: London, Edinburgh, Fort William

BUILT (Mallaig Extension): 1897–1901

FAMOUS FOR: being one of the U.K.'s last sleeper services (Caledonian Sleeper); being pulled by the locomotive used for the Hogwarts Express, on one of the most scenic railways in the world (Jacobite)

EUSTON

DEPARTURES

10

Steph and Andy arrive at Euston Station, central London, just before 9 pm and board the Caledonian Sleeper. An attendant shows them to their compartment with their neatly made beds, but before going to sleep, they decide to head to the lounge car for a snack.

Steph has some Scottish cheeses, but Andy decides to try haggis, a famous Scottish dish made from the heart, liver, and lungs of a sheep mixed with onion, oatmeal, suet and spices, and traditionally stuffed into a sheep's stomach lining. Steph says, "That's disgusting," but Andy is feeling adventurous and thinks it tastes pretty good.

Then it's time for bed, and the slow, rocking movement of the train helps them sleep comfortably through the night.

When they wake up the next morning, dawn is breaking over the Scottish moors. Steph and Andy sip hot tea and watch groups of grouse flying low in the mist and proud stags with large antlers standing silhouetted in the fog. It's a beautiful scene, but nothing compared to what they see after switching to the Jacobite at Fort William.

On arriving in Edinburgh, the capital of Scotland, the Caledonian Sleeper is broken up into sections of cars that are then attached to a different locomotive to take them to their various destinations.

The trip on the Jacobite is only two hours long, but the train—with long trails of white smoke puffing from its engine—runs along the shore of Loch Eil, over the incredible Glenfinnan Viaduct, and across the plains and highlands of Arisaig.

The Glenfinnan Viaduct was completed in 1901. Built from mass concrete, it has 21 arches that each span 50 feet (15 meters).

If it looks like a scene from a movie, that's because it is: the Jacobite played the part of the Hogwarts Express in the *Harry Potter* films and the Glenfinnan Viaduct appeared in four of them.

Snowdon Mountain Railway
Wales's Famous Rack-and-Pinion Railway

Snowdon, the tallest mountain in England and Wales, rises from the ground in northwest Wales to touch the clouds. It's a long way to the top, so more than 100 years ago, it was decided to build a railway that would help visitors get there more easily and see the beautiful view.

Running a train up a steep mountain needs careful engineering, and the Snowdon Mountain Railway keeps its trains safely on track by having a "gripper" rail. This has metal teeth that connect to the underside of the train cars to keep them steady.

COUNTRY: Wales, the U.K.

LENGTH: 4.7 miles (7.6 kilometers)

MAIN STOPS: Llanberis, Clogwyn, Summit

BUILT: 1894–1896

FAMOUS FOR: having the locomotive engine at the end of the carriages

PINION WHEEL

RAIL WHEEL

CENTRAL TOOTHED RAIL

Tracks like this are called rack-and-pinion railways*. Here, Adam sees a diagram showing how the train holds onto these teeth as it makes its way up the mountain. It's a bit like how a metal zipper works!

Snowdon is 3,560 feet (1,085 meters) high. It is one of the most popular mountains for tourists in the U.K.

Unlike with most other railways, the Snowdon train puts its locomotives behind the cars, to push them up the mountain, rather than at the front, where they would have to pull them. Adam thinks this makes sense: surely it's easier to push something uphill in front of you than drag it behind you?

Nowadays, most of the engines are diesel powered, but today they're using an old steam engine, and Adam can see the white smoke and hear the pleasant chugging of the locomotive as it pushes him to the top of the mountain.

Higher up Snowdon, he sees the other peaks of the Snowdonia National Park, including Moel Hebog, which means hill of the falcon in Welsh. It is named that because the peregrine falcon—the world's fastest bird—makes its home in Snowdonia.

Near the start of the line, while still in the foothills*, the train runs over stone bridges and past beautiful waterfalls.

Sitting in the passenger car, Adam sees flocks of sheep in the fields, wild goats balancing deftly on rock crags, and ruins of old stone farmhouses where people lived long ago.

Adam scans the mist covering the mountain and sees no evidence that it lives here, but just as he's about to give up, a falcon swoops downs with great speed, catching a smaller bird in its talons.

Almost as quickly as it appears, the falcon vanishes back into the fog as the train engine continues to puff its way up the mountain.

17

Arctic Circle Train
The Journey to the Northern Lights

The Arctic Circle* freight train has carried mainly industrial loads for more than 100 years. From the famous mine of Kiruna in north Sweden it brings iron ore to shipping boats at the ice-free port of Narvik in Norway. On the return journey, the train carries food: fish and other goods.

Originally built in the early 20th century to haul ore to the Norwegian coast, this route was very important during the Second World War and it still is today. Many people arriving on the passenger train at Kiruna also like to travel on to Rovaniemi, in Finland's Lapland region, which is known as the official hometown of Santa Claus.

The train travels through spectacular scenery. In places that are near the Arctic and Antarctic Circles, the tilt of the Earth as it goes around the Sun means that it is light and dark at strange times during the day. In summer, the Sun sometimes never goes down, even at midnight. In winter, it can be dark all day for more than a month!

Kjerstin's mother is an engineer* on the Arctic Circle train. Every day she drives a freight train between Narvik and Kiruna. Kjerstin loves hearing about her mother's trips so much that, for their winter holiday, her mother is taking her on the Arctic Circle passenger train.

COUNTRY:
Norway, Sweden

LENGTH:
470 miles
(756 kilometers)

MAIN STOPS:
Narvik, Kiruna

STARTED OPERATING:
1902

FAMOUS FOR:
traveling through
far-north
Lapland regions
of Scandinavia

*The northern lights, or aurora borealis, are
a series of colored lights that appear in
the sky. These lights are actually particles
in the air affected by the Earth's magnetic
field and solar winds from the Sun.*

Wrapped up in their cold-weather
clothing, Kjerstin and her mother
board the train at Narvik.

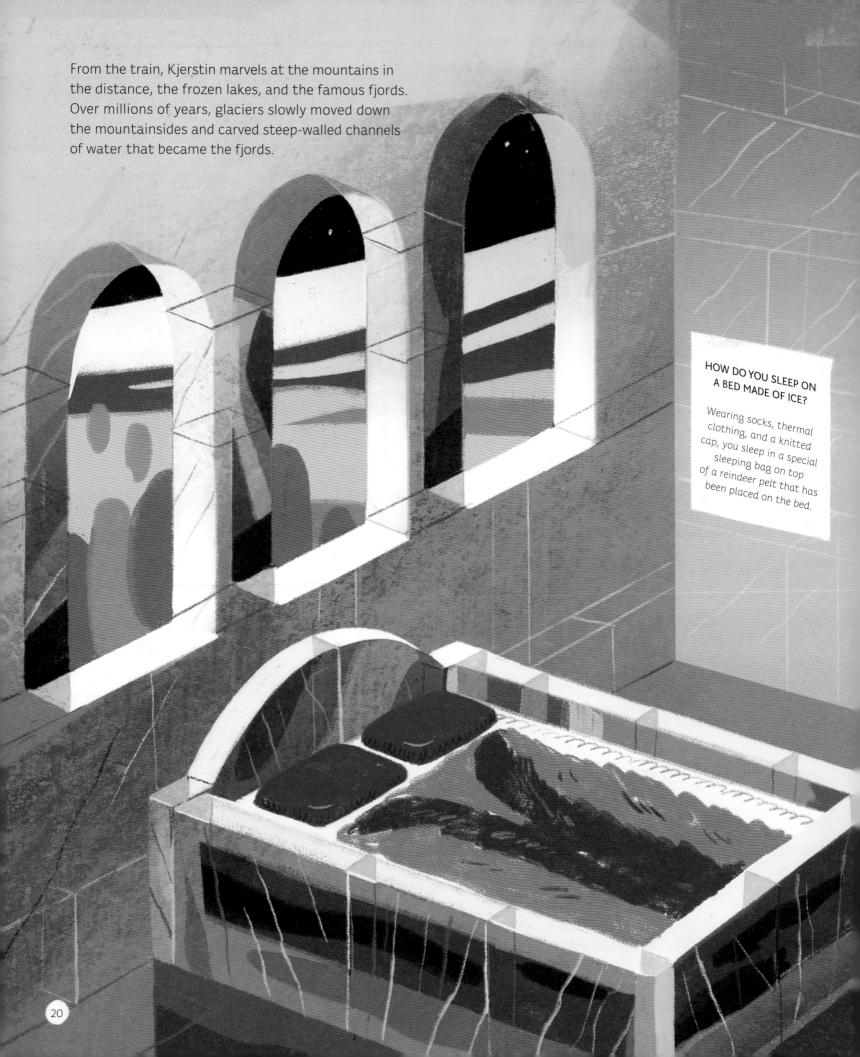

From the train, Kjerstin marvels at the mountains in the distance, the frozen lakes, and the famous fjords. Over millions of years, glaciers slowly moved down the mountainsides and carved steep-walled channels of water that became the fjords.

HOW DO YOU SLEEP ON A BED MADE OF ICE?

Wearing socks, thermal clothing, and a knitted cap, you sleep in a special sleeping bag on top of a reindeer pelt that has been placed on the bed.

After crossing into Sweden, Kjerstin and her mother stop at Kiruna, where they will spend the night nearby at the famous Icehotel. Everything here—including the beds—is made of ice! Because it's winter, the sky is dark, even though it's only the afternoon. Luckily for Kjerstin and her mother, the northern lights soon make an appearance and dance in the sky.

The lights follow them the next day, when they continue into Finland, to the town of Rovaniemi. This part of Finland is sometimes called Lapland, but it is known to the native Sámi people—famous for their skill of reindeer herding—as Sápmi.

Many of the buildings in this region have steep, pointy roofs to stop too much snow piling up on top of them.

Kjerstin can see some of the Sámi people driving reindeer sleds toward the SnowCastle in Kemi. In fact, according to some legends, Santa Claus and his famous team of reindeers live in Rovaniemi!

WISH LIST

Before she and her mother head home to Norway, Kjerstin drops her wish list off at the Santa Claus Main Post Office. It's in Santa Claus Village, just a few miles north of Rovaniemi.

Namibia Desert Express
An African Safari by Train

The Namibia Desert Express is a sightseeing train ride that lasts several days as it travels across the sublime desert landscape of this southern-African country. There are multiple stops along the way and passengers are able to enjoy fun activities and incredible sights during their journey.

Giraffes use their necks when dueling one another for dominance.

Local fruits include the spiny !Nara melon (the exclamation point is a clicking sound in the Khoekhoe language) and the Kavango lemon, also called a monkey orange—a hard fruit filled with sweet and sour pulp and seeds.*

A trip on the Namibia Desert Express is a true adventure, as it gives you the opportunity to spot lots of animals along the route. One of the stops is for a safari drive in Jeeps, during which you can see giraffes and zebras drinking at watering holes (while always keeping an eye out for wild dogs that might attack them).

As a birthday treat, Sonu has booked a cabin for herself on the train. Soon Windhoek is behind her and she enjoys the safari a lot. She sees herds of wildebeest, moving together as though they share a common purpose. To her, they look like powerful, muscular wild cows.

The Namaqua chameleon can "drink" water and nighttime dew through the scales on its body—a good skill to have in a hot desert.

Back on the train, Sonu is served a dinner of springbok steak, which is an African antelope, along with a traditional local porridge made from mashed millet called mahangu.

Night falls across the wide savanna and the sky is full of stars. Two jackals howl in the distance, occasionally talking to each other with short yelps and warning other animals away from their territory.

Sonu plays a game of chess with a fellow passenger. The train's chessboard is special: the board and pieces are made of the colorful mineral sands of the Namib desert.

The next morning, after coffee and breakfast, Sonu and the other passengers leave the train to walk up a giant sand dune. From its top they can see the Atlantic Ocean shimmering in the heat. Afterwards, the Desert Express takes them to the coastal city of Swakopmund.

The train will gently carry them across a vast, empty land where, due to the arid conditions and frequent sandstorms, it's not possible for people to live, delivering them to a peaceful town found between the desert and the sea.

The train stops at night, sometimes for a fireside gathering of the passengers. It resumes its journey each morning.

Mountain Railways of India

The "Miniature" Toy Trains of Darjeeling, Nilgiri, and Shimla

Imagine small, toy-like trains that follow winding routes on narrow tracks through the stunning scenery of the Indian mountains via picturesque tunnels and bridges, and you're there! These "toy trains" have a long history with many influences.

During the 19th century, India was part of the British Empire, which meant that Indians didn't rule their own country—it was controlled by the British, who made money by selling India's resources, such as tea and spices. Summer on the hot Indian plains around the city of Delhi or in the humid port hubs of Bombay and Calcutta was far too uncomfortable for people used to the cool, rainy weather of the U.K.

To make work in the mountains easier, the British and their engineers—many of them Scottish—decided to build railways. They had already built many railroads elsewhere, perfect for crossing flat land, carrying freight, civilian passengers, soldiers, and mail. But for the high and winding paths into the foothills of the Himalayas and Nilgiri mountains, more advanced engineering was needed.

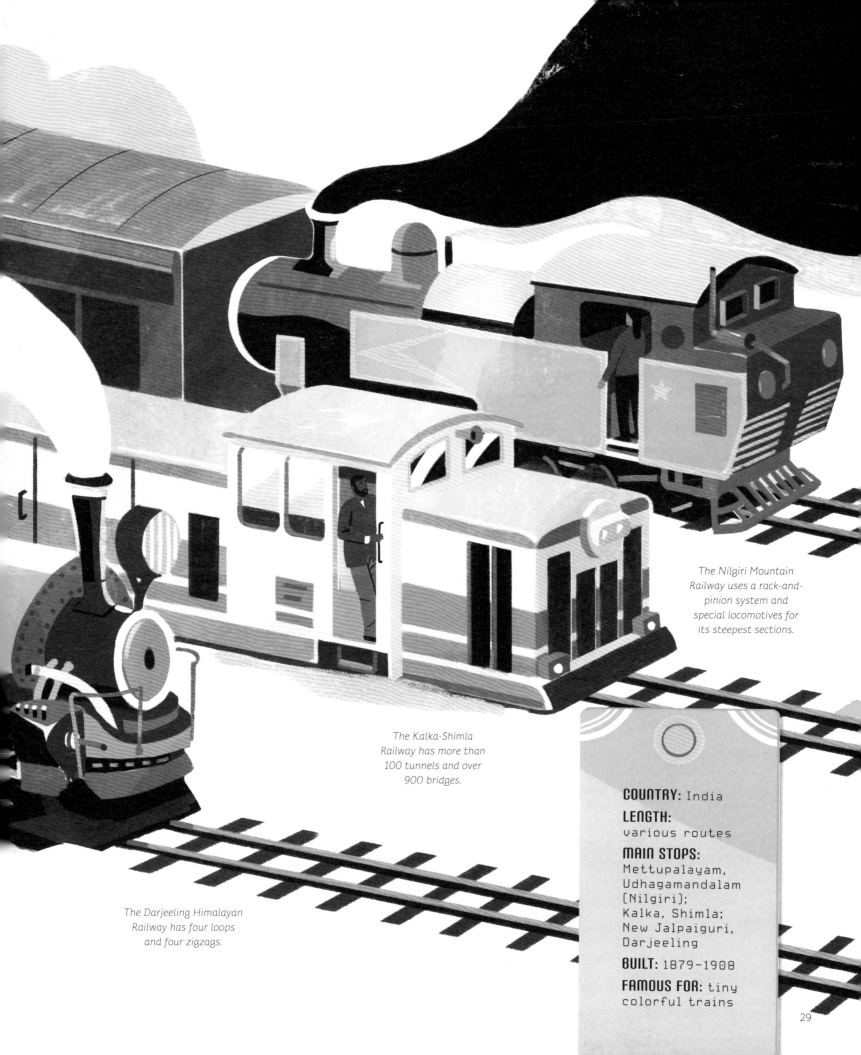

The Nilgiri Mountain Railway uses a rack-and-pinion system and special locomotives for its steepest sections.

The Kalka-Shimla Railway has more than 100 tunnels and over 900 bridges.

The Darjeeling Himalayan Railway has four loops and four zigzags.

COUNTRY: India

LENGTH: various routes

MAIN STOPS: Mettupalayam, Udhagamandalam (Nilgiri); Kalka, Shimla; New Jalpaiguri, Darjeeling

BUILT: 1879-1908

FAMOUS FOR: tiny colorful trains

So they built three beautiful mountain railways on very narrow gauges—2ft (60 centimeters) wide, almost a third of the width of that used with a standard train—earning them the nickname toy trains. The passenger cars are only 7 feet (2.1 meters) wide—not much wider than most automobiles!

The tracks bend through tunnels and across viaduct bridges, making long loops as a way of reducing the steep inclines and winding their way past interestingly named locations such as Agony Point and Sensation Corner.

The Agony Point loop got its name because it is the sharpest turn on the Darjeeling Himalayan Railway.

Today, all three railroads are recognized by the United Nations as World Heritage Sites*, and are mainly used by passengers, although they still carry some mail.

They end their journeys up in the tea fields of Nilgiri and Darjeeling and in the pretty hill town of Shimla, the bustling capital of the state of Himachal Pradesh.

Darjeeling tea is famous for its delicate flavor and floral aroma. It is picked by hand on hillside tea estates.

Snacks are an important part of the Indian railway experience. During his summer vacation from school, Virraj helps his father sell chai tea and snacks to passengers traveling on the Kalka-Shimla Railway.

His mother and father wake up early in the morning to make samosas and chai.

The tea leaves to make the chai are sometimes brought down the mountains by the railways.

Chai, a sweet milky tea.

Samosa, a crispy fried snack made with vegetables.

Virraj and his father only have a few minutes to work once the trains stop. Expertly carrying the tea on metal trays without spilling it, they run up to the carriages and along the train.

They have to compete with other vendors, all shouting, "Chai!" and "Samosas!" Passengers hand money to them in exchange for the food and drink, and after just a few minutes, the train is off to its next station.

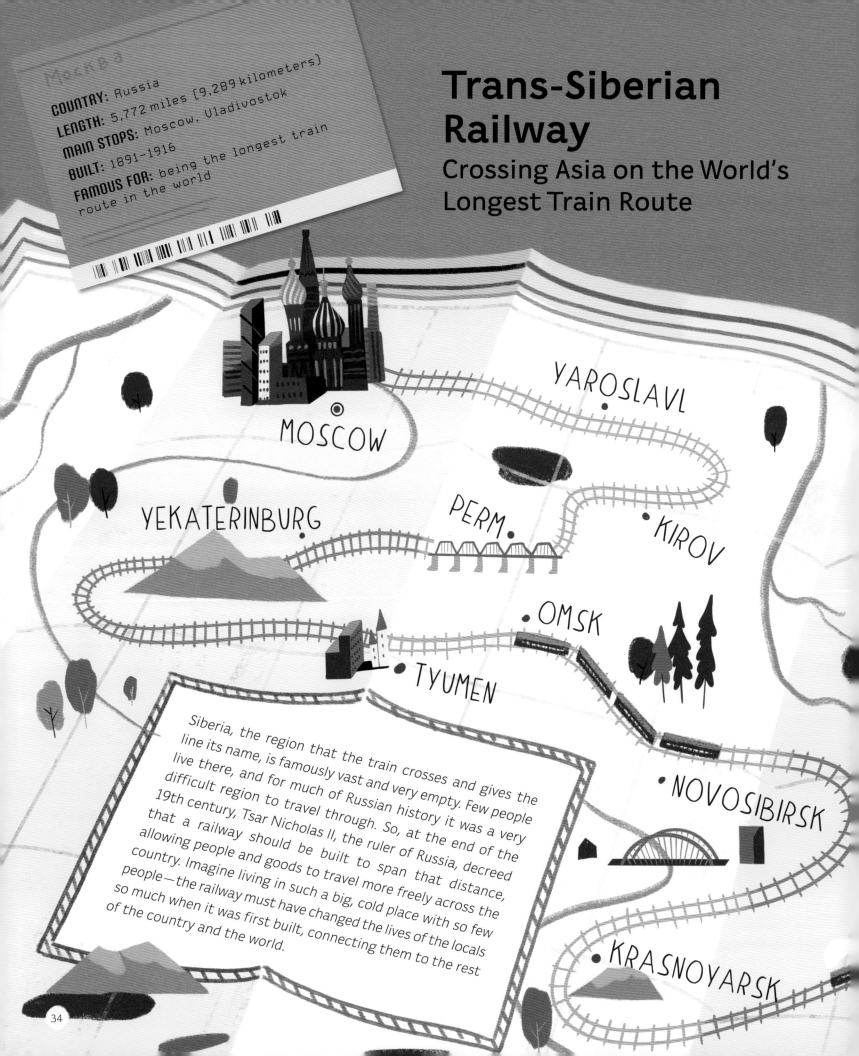

Trans-Siberian Railway
Crossing Asia on the World's Longest Train Route

YAROSLAVL

MOSCOW

YEKATERINBURG

PERM

KIROV

OMSK

TYUMEN

NOVOSIBIRSK

KRASNOYARSK

Siberia, the region that the train crosses and gives the line its name, is famously vast and very empty. Few people live there, and for much of Russian history it was a very difficult region to travel through. So, at the end of the 19th century, Tsar Nicholas II, the ruler of Russia, decreed that a railway should be built to span that distance, allowing people and goods to travel more freely across the country. Imagine living in such a big, cold place with so few people—the railway must have changed the lives of the locals so much when it was first built, connecting them to the rest of the country and the world.

The Trans-Siberian Railway is a very famous railway, mainly because it is the longest train route in the world—more than 5,000 miles (8,047 kilometers), almost twice as wide as the United States! In addition to carrying travelers, the Trans-Siberian is part of a very important freight corridor for transporting goods from the Far East into Europe and vice versa.

The railway plays an important role in the life and economy of Russia and her neighboring countries. In Moscow, the capital of Russia, freight containers are unloaded from trains that travel on this route; some are bound for warehouses in the city, others travel further on by truck, boat, or another train.

The map shows how the train travels all the way across Russia. It also has extensions into the countries of China, Mongolia, and North Korea.

KHABAROVSK

VLADIVOSTOK

BIROBIDZHAN

IRKUTSK

ULAN-UDE

TAYSHET

CHITA

The Trans-Siberian Railway is such a long line that it spans eight time zones*. It means that when it's lunchtime in Moscow, kids in Vladivostok go to sleep.

Rafi is part of a youth group visiting Russia to learn about its culture and history. He and a few other children are being taken on a section of the Trans-Siberian Railway. He can't believe how long it is.

Passengers are likely to be served borscht while eating in the dining car. The main ingredient of this Russian soup is traditionally beet-root, which gives it a bright red color. It is usually served with dollops of sour cream, and during the summer, some people prefer to eat a chilled version.

This railway crosses so many regions—imagine how many different accents and languages you might hear while traveling on the Trans-Siberian!

Shinkansen (Bullet Train)
The Original High-Speed Train

The first shinkansen train line was built in 1964, just in time for Japan to host that year's summer Olympic Games. It was the first high-speed railway in the world, traveling between the cities of Tokyo and Osaka, and its trains' incredible speed and sleek, aerodynamic design earned them the nickname shinkansen, or bullet train.

COUNTRY: Japan
LENGTH: various routes
MAIN STOPS: many cities all over Japan
BUILT: 1964
FAMOUS FOR: being the world's first high-speed train

The most amazing element of the shinkansen's speedy design is its long and slender "nose," which helps it move faster through the air in its path.

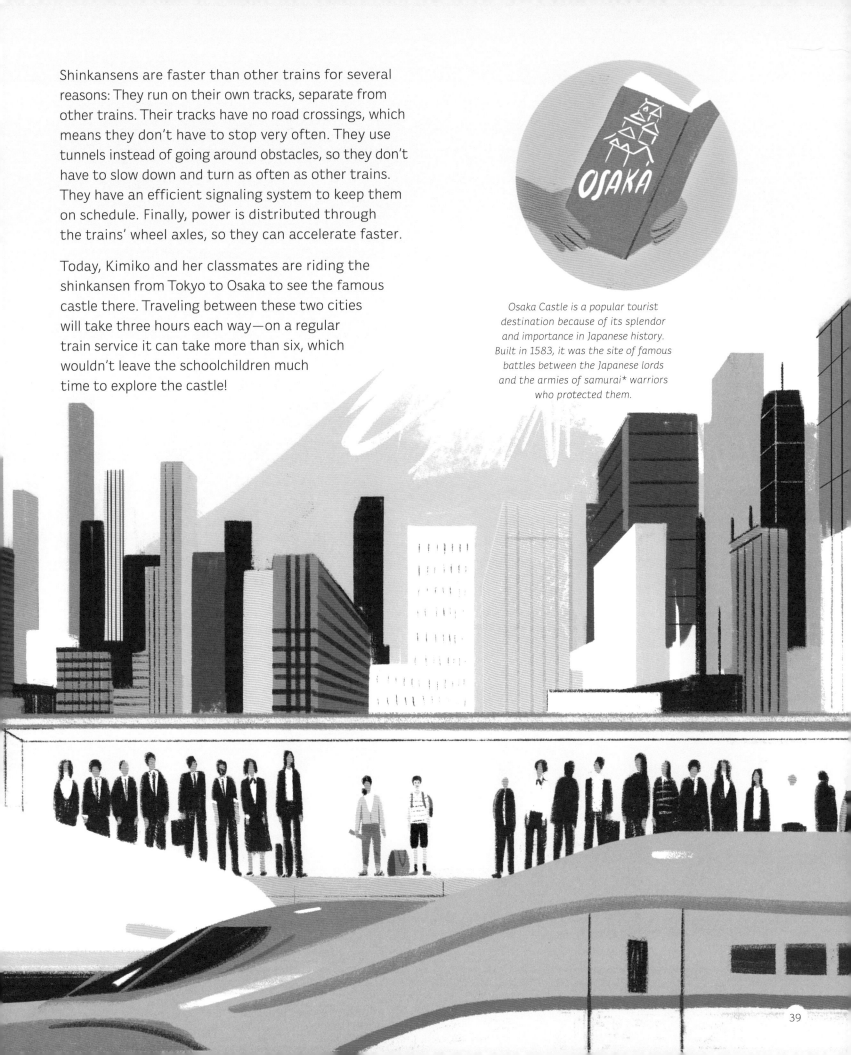

Shinkansens are faster than other trains for several reasons: They run on their own tracks, separate from other trains. Their tracks have no road crossings, which means they don't have to stop very often. They use tunnels instead of going around obstacles, so they don't have to slow down and turn as often as other trains. They have an efficient signaling system to keep them on schedule. Finally, power is distributed through the trains' wheel axles, so they can accelerate faster.

Today, Kimiko and her classmates are riding the shinkansen from Tokyo to Osaka to see the famous castle there. Traveling between these two cities will take three hours each way—on a regular train service it can take more than six, which wouldn't leave the schoolchildren much time to explore the castle!

Osaka Castle is a popular tourist destination because of its splendor and importance in Japanese history. Built in 1583, it was the site of famous battles between the Japanese lords and the armies of samurai* warriors who protected them.

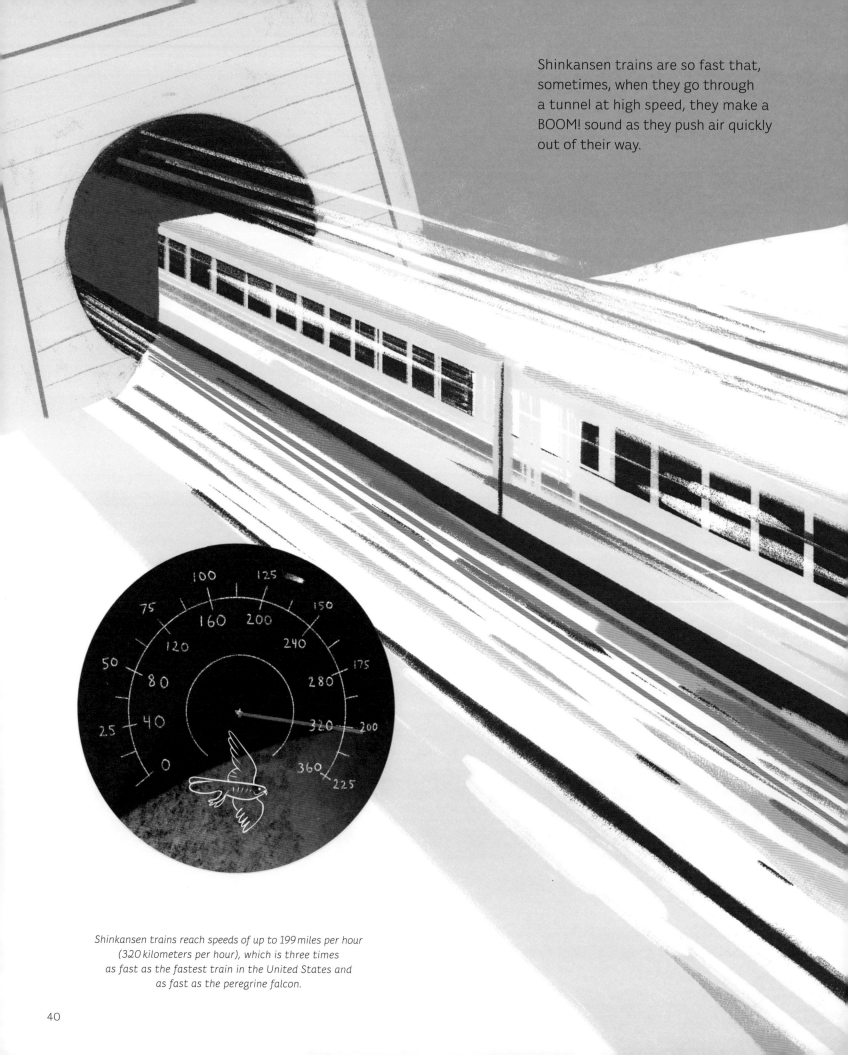

Shinkansen trains are so fast that, sometimes, when they go through a tunnel at high speed, they make a BOOM! sound as they push air quickly out of their way.

Shinkansen trains reach speeds of up to 199 miles per hour (320 kilometers per hour), which is three times as fast as the fastest train in the United States and as fast as the peregrine falcon.

Even though Japan is a country that sometimes has earthquakes, Kimiko feels safe because shinkansens have an earthquake-detection system that will automatically stop the trains in an emergency. This is how it works:

Seismographs—devices that can detect vibrations in the ground—are set up around the country.

When the system detects the first movements of an earthquake, automatic safety brakes are triggered, often with only a few seconds to spare.

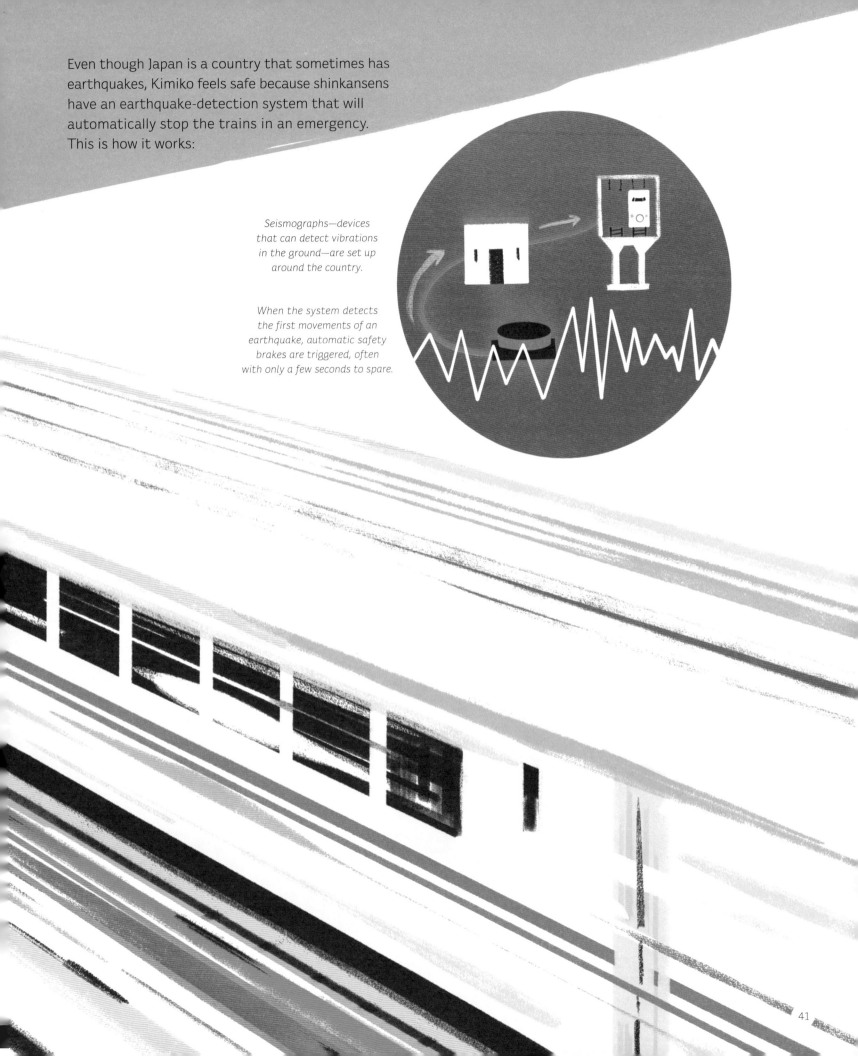

Kimiko can see the snow-topped peak of Mount Fuji from the window as she eats the food in her bento that she bought from a vendor on the train.

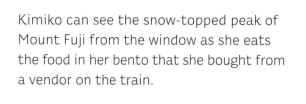

Some foods popular in bentos are rice, fish cakes, sushi, and pickled fruits and vegetables. Sometimes they also include a sweet dessert such as a red bean bun.

Mount Fuji is 12,389 feet (3,776 meters) high. It is a famous symbol of Japan and appears in a lot of traditional and modern artwork.

A bento is a traditional boxed meal in Japan that is small, portable, and easy to buy at many locations. The boxes sold at train stations and on trains are called *ekiben*, and they are often filled with delicacies from the region the station is in. Some boxes are highly decorated—sometimes they're shaped like trains or stations—and are collected as souvenirs.

Today, there is a whole network of high-speed shinkansen trains connecting Japan's major cities, and millions of children like Kimiko can travel as fast as a peregrine falcon!

The Ghan
The First Train to Cross the Wild Australian Outback

Australia is a very big country—so big that if you travel across it you can experience several climates. It's almost like having different seasons in one day! The Ghan takes its passengers all the way from the southern city of Adelaide to Darwin in the north—a trip of 1,851 miles (2,979 km).

There are great sections of sparsely populated plains, savanna, and desert in the middle of the country, which are commonly known as the outback. More than a century ago, when the cities of Adelaide and Darwin were first built and began to grow, the enormous distance between them, which included sometimes-dangerous and unmapped regions, became a problem for travelers. Crossing it was considered a feat for only the bravest explorers.

Miri is traveling through Australia on the Ghan. According to a sign at the train station, if she had been making her journey 150 years ago, she would only have been able to cross large portions of the outback by riding in a caravan* of camels, animals better suited to the dry desert climate than horses.

COUNTRY: Australia
LENGTH: 1,851 miles (2,979 kilometers)
MAIN STOPS: Adelaide, Alice Springs, Darwin
BUILT: 1878–1929
FAMOUS FOR: connecting the south and north coasts through the Australian outback

To lead these camel caravans, Australians hired drivers from Afghanistan who were familiar with the animals. When these caravans were finally replaced by a train, it was called the Afghan Express in their honor. Because Australians love nicknames, this was eventually shortened to the Ghan.

Miri can picture how difficult such a long trip through the desert would have been for the camel caravans, especially if the riders didn't know what they would find along the way. She's getting thirsty just thinking about it!

Today the Ghan is a popular tourist train, and during the 54-hour journey, Miri sees descendants of those original camels roaming free across the outback with native animals such as kangaroos, emus, and wallabies.

Miri is spending a few nights at the trip's halfway stop: Alice Springs, a town that was only able to grow and survive because of the railway line being built through it.

Miri is putting on sunscreen, a hat, and insect repellent to protect herself against the elements.

In the heart of Australia, known nowadays as the Red Center, the iron in the soil turns the earth and sand dunes a beautiful shade of red.

THE GHAN

1102

Kangaroos—and their smaller cousins wallabies—are large, hopping mammals that are only native to Australia. They have become a famous symbol of the country.

The emu is the second-tallest bird in the world, after the ostrich. They can't fly, but they can run up to 35 miles per hour (56 kilometers per hour).

The famous sacred rock mountain Uluru can be found in the Red Center.

Aboriginal Australians—the native peoples who lived on the continent before European colonization— such as the Arrernte and Anangu, have lived in the region for more than 50,000 years, long before the railroad was ever built!

Australia is in the southern hemisphere* of the globe. Here, you can see perfect night skies filled with thousands of stars, and after two nights of stargazing in the remote town of Alice Springs—a good place to explore the Red Center from—Miri is back on the Ghan.

As she gets closer to Darwin, the scenery becomes more green, with forests, orchards, and mangrove trees curling up from the banks of the Elizabeth River. Miri is amazed at the lush tropical environment of Darwin—it seems a whole world away from the burning desert she has just crossed.

Rocky Mountaineer
A Journey Through the Wilderness of Western Canada

If you love wildlife, book a ticket to travel on the Rocky Mountaineer in Western Canada. Animals that can often be seen from the train include grizzly and black bears, mountain goats, elks, and eagles—sometimes the train will even slow down so you can get a better view.

COUNTRY:
Canada

LENGTH:
various routes

MAIN STOPS:
Vancouver, Banff, Jasper

STARTED OPERATING: 1990

FAMOUS FOR:
views of the plants, animals, and landscapes of Western Canada

The Rocky Mountaineer has glass-domed coaches and outdoor viewing areas between cars. It is staffed by hosts who provide information about what passengers can see out the window and serves gourmet meals made using local ingredients such as Fraser River salmon. But the most spectacular thing about taking a journey on this train is the rugged Canadian wilderness it crosses.

Unforgettable places and sights include the Great Bear Rainforest, which has 1,000-year-old Pacific red cedar trees and Sitka spruce trees that are more than 295 feet (90 meters) tall growing in it; Pyramid Creek Falls waterfall, whose waters flow right under the train tracks; Jasper, which has been designated a large dark sky preserve*, making it the perfect place for viewing the stars at night; and Fraser Canyon, where tens of thousands of people came to seek their fortune when a gold rush* started in the area in 1858.

Fir

Pine

Western hemlock

Pacific red cedar

Evergreen fir, pine, and hemlock trees drop and spread their needles and cones, carpeting the forest floor.

Sisters Willa and Oona love animals, so they are very excited about taking a trip on the Rocky Mountaineer. During the day they see some smaller mammals: beavers building a dam, a jackrabbit enjoying some tasty leaves, a red fox slinking through the shrubs, and a raccoon.

Overhead, they can see the last of the season's Canada geese migrating to the warmer south for the winter, their black heads and necks stretched out far ahead of their wide wings.

Canada geese

Elk

Bald eagle

Grizzly bear

Black bear

Looking up through the glass dome of the car of the train
with her binoculars, Willa sees a bald eagle flying overhead.
Oona snaps a photo of an adult elk with enormous antlers
that she sees through a clearing in the trees. It's even
possible to spot different bears along the route.

Alaska Railroad
America's Last Flag-stop Trains

Alaska is the largest state in the United States—it's twice as big as Texas. It's also the farthest west and the farthest north, and is separated from most of the rest of the country by Canada. When you're here, you can travel on the Alaska Railroad, which makes its way through the state's beautiful wilderness, and take a ride on one of America's last flag-stop services, the Hurricane Turn. This means you can make the trains stop yourself!

COUNTRY:
the United States

LENGTH:
470 miles
(756 kilometers)

MAIN STOPS:
Fairbanks, Denali,
Anchorage, Seward

BUILT:
1914–1923

FAMOUS FOR:
flag-stop service

The moose is the largest member of the deer family. The males have antlers that can grow to have a span of more than 5 feet (1.5 meters).

It's mainly freight trains that run on the Alaska Railroad, but its most famous passenger service is one named the Hurricane Turn. This travels from the southern part of the state, where it's more populous, into the wilder, less-populated north. People can sit in a glass-domed observation car and look out as the famed blue and yellow train leaves the towns and cities behind.

The railroad travels through areas where there are no towns or cities—in some places there aren't even any roads! Of course, that means there are also no train stations. So how does the Hurricane Turn know where to stop? Since this is a flag-stop service, people can get on or off the train anywhere along the route they want. When they need to get on, they just have to wave at the train from near the side of the track—it's almost like hailing a taxi!

Aretta and her parents are visiting Alaska this summer, when the northern snows have melted and wildflowers can be seen across the land. From the train they can see Denali, the highest mountain in North America, whose summit is an impressive 20,310 feet (6,190 meters) above sea level.

Denali used to be named Mount McKinley, after an American president, but following decades of advocacy* by indigenous* groups, its original, native name was made official.

In winter, once passengers get off the train, they often have to continue their journeys by snowmobile—sometimes even by dog sled.

Rare sights to be seen on the journey include kermode bears—they're a subspecies of the American black bear but some of them are born with white fur!

Aretta's parents are taking her camping in a cabin in the woods for a few days. When it's time to go home they will return to the train tracks and wait for the southbound Hurricane Turn.

Aretta and her parents go early to the train tracks so they don't miss their ride. They pick a spot where the engineer will be able to see them waving from a distance.

"How can we hop on?"

"By waving this!"

"That's why it's called a flag stop."

56

The train sees Aretta waving her towel and stops to let her family on.

"Is it strange to see people waving towels at the train?"

"Not really—usually they wave T-shirts!"

57

COUNTRY: Peru

LENGTH:
Cusco to Machu
Picchu, 67 miles
(108 kilometers)

MAIN STOPS:
Cusco, Machu
Picchu

BUILT: 1907-1928

FAMOUS FOR:
taking visitors
to the ancient
ruins of Machu
Picchu

PeruRail
The Trains of Peru's Scenic Andes Mountains

Peru's most famous landmark is the ruins of Machu Picchu, a city high in the Andes mountains that was home to the people of the Incan civilization more than 500 years ago. To get there, you can hike up the mountain or take a bus, but many people love to go by train.

Peru has many famous railways, built across the dramatic and beautiful landscapes of the Andes mountains. Its Ferrovias Central railway is the second highest in the world after the Qinghai-Tibet railway in China.

Most of the country's trains carry freight, especially minerals from the many mines in the area, but passenger trains do occasionally run on freight tracks, and are an excellent way to see the natural beauty of the country. Several go daily from Cusco to Machu Picchu.

BINGHAM

Aysén lives in Cusco. She has friends visiting from Europe and she would like to take them to see Machu Picchu. They want to take a train, but which one?

59

Tickets for the blue and gold Hiram Bingham train are quite expensive because it is so luxurious, so Aysén and her friends take another train instead. They have an amazing view as it makes its way back and forth up the narrow-gauge railway known locally as El Zig-Zag until it reaches the stop for the ancient ruins of Machu Picchu.

The standard tourist trains have comfortable seats and regular windows, but Aysén and her friends travel on a service that is made up of glass-domed observation cars. They look out all around them as their train climbs the mountain.

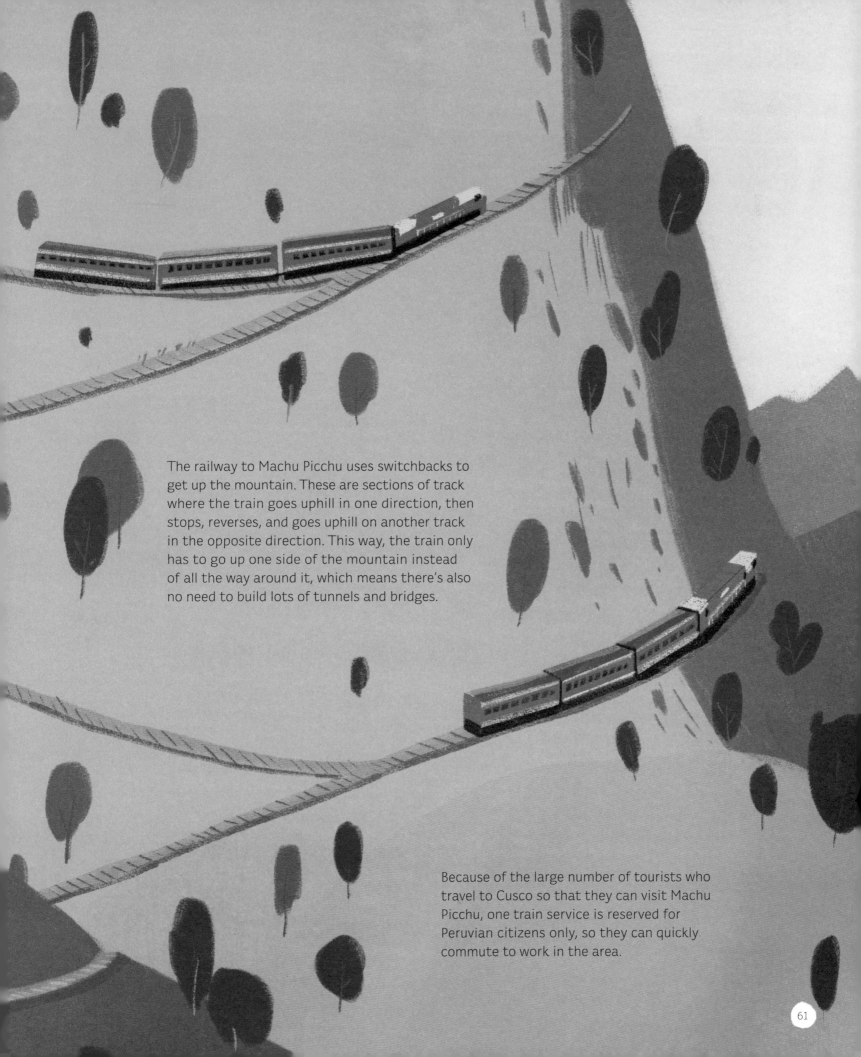

The railway to Machu Picchu uses switchbacks to get up the mountain. These are sections of track where the train goes uphill in one direction, then stops, reverses, and goes uphill on another track in the opposite direction. This way, the train only has to go up one side of the mountain instead of all the way around it, which means there's also no need to build lots of tunnels and bridges.

Because of the large number of tourists who travel to Cusco so that they can visit Machu Picchu, one train service is reserved for Peruvian citizens only, so they can quickly commute to work in the area.

"Next time let's take the Hiram Bingham!"
Aysén's friends say.

The Hiram Bingham is a very fancy train named after the American explorer who rediscovered the ruins of Machu Picchu in the early 20th century. It has an observation car with an outdoor platform so you can feel the mountain air on your face as you travel, and there is a band on board that plays Peruvian songs.

The city of Machu Picchu was built high in the Andes mountains by the Inca people in the 15th century. The Incas were a civilization of people indigenous to South America who built cities and ruled over large parts of the continent.

New York & Atlantic Railway
The Railroad that Supplies New York City

New York City is famous for its vast and complicated subway system, but there's one train line operating there that most New Yorkers have never heard of— the New York & Atlantic Railway. Instead of carrying people, its trains transport important goods around the city.

In the early morning, big shipping containers full of goods are loaded onto barges at the port in Jersey City.

Once the containers are safely on board, the ships carry them across New York Bay, past the Statue of Liberty and the other boats, to the New York & Atlantic Railway terminal on the Brooklyn waterfront, at the west end of Long Island.

COUNTRY: the United States
LENGTH: 270 miles (435 kilometers)
MAIN STOPS: Brooklyn, Long Island
STARTED OPERATING: 1997
FAMOUS FOR: carrying goods that make the big city safer and more enjoyable

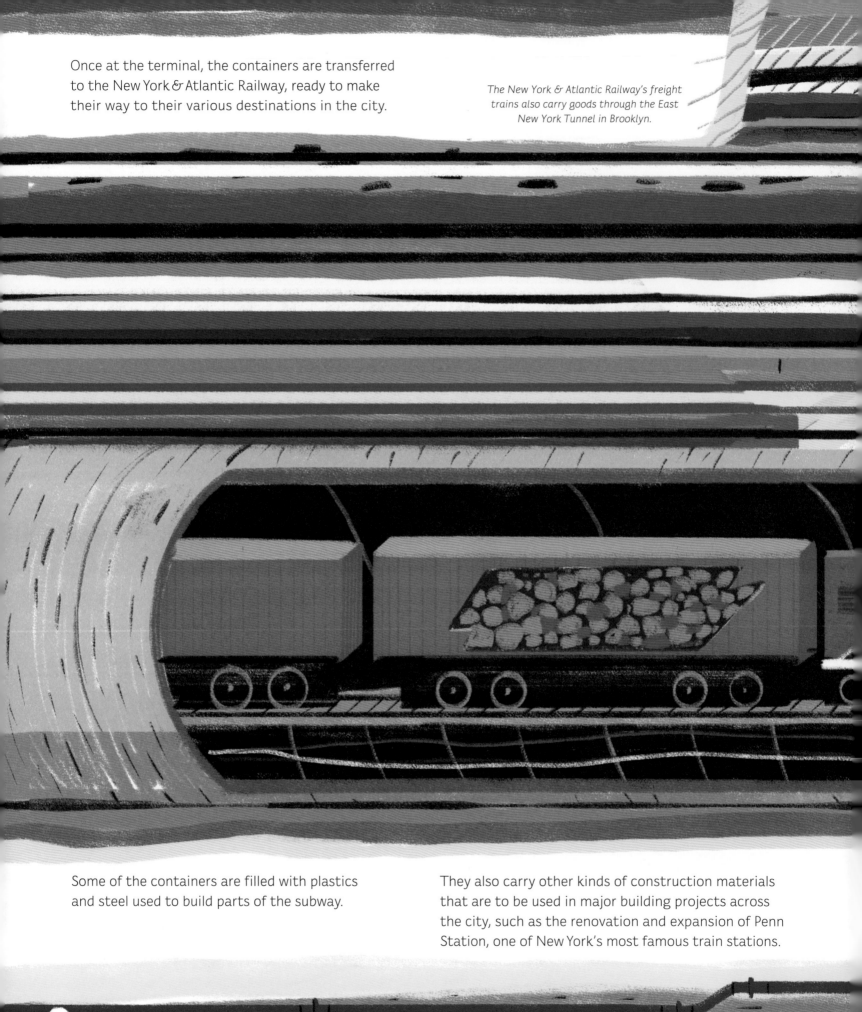

Once at the terminal, the containers are transferred to the New York & Atlantic Railway, ready to make their way to their various destinations in the city.

The New York & Atlantic Railway's freight trains also carry goods through the East New York Tunnel in Brooklyn.

Some of the containers are filled with plastics and steel used to build parts of the subway.

They also carry other kinds of construction materials that are to be used in major building projects across the city, such as the renovation and expansion of Penn Station, one of New York's most famous train stations.

Other goods being transported include food, paper products, sand, minerals, stone, clay, glass, and fuel.

Arlo and his father have also come to Long Island from Jersey City, but they are here to enjoy the county fair. After getting off the subway, they take a passenger train that travels on the Long Island Rail Road, which shares some of its tracks with the New York & Atlantic Railway.

At the fairground there are lots of things that have arrived here by the same route...

The hot dogs and ice cream that Arlo and his father enjoy were brought here by the New York & Atlantic Railway.

The fuel used to cook the food is carried on the railway, too.

So was the gravel beneath their feet.

The french fries and onion rings traveled along the same tracks.

And the meat used for the hamburgers.

And even the recycled cardboard packaging!

Glossary

Advocacy This is when someone publicly supports or recommends a particular cause, policy, or proposal that they feel is important. Climate-change advocates call for businesses to be careful about causing greenhouse-gas emissions and campaign for governments to bring in laws that will protect the planet.

Arctic Circle Like the equator, this is an imaginary line that circles the Earth. Above it is the northernmost region of the planet, where the weather is often a lot colder than in the rest of the world. The eight countries that have land within the Arctic Circle are Norway, Sweden, Finland, Russia, the United States (Alaska), Canada, Denmark (Greenland), and Iceland.

Caravan A group of people and animals or vehicles that travel together. Historically, caravans were mainly used to cross desert areas, often to sell goods such as fabrics, spices, and jewelry in other parts of the country or world.

Dark sky preserve An area where artificial-light pollution, which can be caused by things such as streetlights, is restricted. Having a dark sky preserve in place means that activity in the night skies and the star constellations are much clearer to see.

Engineer A train engineer is the person who operates, or is in charge of, a train and its engine. They are also sometimes called the train driver or locomotive driver.

Foothill A lower slope or low hill at the bottom of a mountain or mountain range.

Freight Goods such as food, machinery, medical supplies—anything!—that are transported around the world by trains, trucks, ships, and airplanes.

Gauge The spacing of the rails on a railway track. Narrow-gauge tracks are used when there are space restrictions, like in the mountainous parts of India; wider gauges are used where the land is flatter and larger amounts of passengers and freight need to be carried.

Gold rush The rush of people to new places where gold has been discovered in the hope of getting rich. Many big gold rushes happened in the 19th century, in countries such as Australia, Canada, and the United States.

Indigenous People or things that are native to, or belong to, the country where they are found. Today's indigenous peoples are the descendants of those who lived in a country or region at a time when people from different cultures arrived and brought with them new traditions and social, cultural, economic, and political structures that then became dominant in daily life. Indigenous peoples have held on to their own languages, traditions, and values, and have important knowledge about how best to live on and manage the land around them.

Khoekhoe A language spoken in southern Africa, including by the Topnaar people of Namibia, whose main staple food is the !Nara melon. Like many languages of southern Africa, Khoekhoe uses mouth clicks for some consonants—a similar kind of sound you might know is the one people make for the "clip-clop" of a horse's hooves.

Locomotive The large vehicle that pulls—or, in some cases, pushes—the cars of a railway train. It gets the power to do this from fuel, which can be wood or coal (as seen with steam locomotives) or diesel, or from electricity, which can come from an overhead line, an extra rail in the tracks, or an onboard battery.

Rack-and-pinion railway A system used on steep railways where the tracks have an additional, toothed rail, usually in the middle. Special cog wheels, or pinions, fitted on the bottom of the trains attach to this rack, helping the trains to climb the tracks.

Samurai A member of a powerful class of warriors in Japan whose history can be traced from the 12th century to the 1870s, when they were abolished by the new emperor and government. Samurais protected the country's landholders and, in times of peace, looked after their estates. They were allowed to carry weapons, even when walking about in town, and were famous for their unswerving loyalty and refusal to acknowledge pain.

Southern hemisphere The half of the Earth that lies south of the equator—the imaginary line that goes round the middle of the Earth. There is more ocean in this half of the world than in the northern hemisphere and the weather is usually warmer.

Time zone While it may be daytime where you are, for someone on the opposite side of the planet it will be night, as they are facing away from the Sun. The idea of time zones is to divide the world into segments, and for everyone in each zone to set their clocks to the same hour. Most zones are an hour different from the one next to them. Some very large countries, such as the United States, have more than one time zone.

Viaduct A long, high bridge made of several arches that carries a railway or a road across a valley, body of water, or busy town center. Mountain railways often use them to cross tricky terrain.

World Heritage Sites Natural or manmade areas or structures that are so important they are given this special protection by the United Nations so that future generations will be able to enjoy them, too. Examples include Uluru in Australia and the three railways used by the toy trains in India.

Tales of the Rails
Legendary Train Routes of the World

Illustrated by Ryan Johnson
Written by Nathaniel Adams

This book was conceived, edited, and designed by gestalten.

Edited by Maria-Elisabeth Niebius and Robert Klanten

Design and layout by Emily Sear

Typefaces: Karlo Sans by Sofie Beier, Carbon by Ray Larabie

Printed by Gutenberg Beuys Feindruckerei GmbH, Langenhagen
Made in Germany

Published by Little Gestalten, Berlin, 2020
ISBN 978-3-89955-845-6

For more information, and to order books, please visit www.little.gestalten.com.

Bibliographic information published by the Deutsche Nationalbibliothek. The Deutsche
Nationalbibliothek lists this publication in the Deutsche Nationalbibliografie; detailed
bibliographic data are available online at www.dnb.de.

This book was printed on paper certified according to the standards of the FSC®.